Salvage at Twilight

DAN BURT was born in South Philadelphia, read English at St John's College, Cambridge and attended Yale Law School. A lawyer and businessman, his poetry and prose have appeared in *Poetry Review*, *PN Review*, *TLS*, *The Financial Times*, *The New Statesman*, *The Sunday Times*, *Granta*, *Commonweal*, *Clutag Five Poems Series*, *The Forward Book of Poetry* (best poems of 2013), *The Poetry of Sex* (Penguin Anthology), *The Institute News Letter* (Institute for Advanced Study), *Courtauld News*, and *New Poetries V* (2011) amongst others. Two chapbooks, *Searched For Text* (2008) and *Certain Windows* (2011) were published by Lintott/Carcanet Press, as well as a collaboration, *Cold Eye*, with artist Paul Hodgson (Marlborough Graphics/Lintott Press, 2010). Carcanet published *We Look Like This*, a collected edition of his poetry and prose, in May 2012. Notting Hill Editions published the UK edition of his memoir, *You Think It Strange*, in 2014, and Overlook Press the US edition in 2015. The Poetry Archive has twice recorded him reading his work. He lives and writes in London and St. John's College, Cambridge, of which he is an Honorary Fellow.

DAN BURT

Salvage at Twilight

CARCANET

Acknowledgments

Some of the poems in this book were previously published in *Bateau, Commonweal, Clutag Five Poems Series, The Eagle, Johnian Poetry, Newsletter of the Institute for Advanced Study, New Poetry V, Paula Rego 80th Birthday Tribute* (A Rudolf publication), *Poetry Archive, PN Review,* and the *Times Literary Supplement.*

First published in Great Britain in 2019 by
Carcanet Press Ltd
Alliance House, 30 Cross Street
Manchester M2 7AQ
www.carcanet.co.uk

A CIP catalogue record for this book is available from the British Library.
Paperback ISBN 978 1 78410 791 8
Hardback ISBN 978 1 78410 922 6

The publisher acknowledges financial assistance from Arts Council England.

Typeset in England by XL Publishing Services, Exmouth
Printed and bound in England by SRP Ltd, Exeter

Contents

Slag

Practice

Contrasts

Salvages

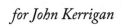

for John Kerrigan

'God save thee, ancient Mariner!
From the fiends, that plague thee thus! –
Why look'st thou so?' – With my cross bow
I shot the Albatross.

The Rime Of The Ancient Mariner
Samuel Taylor Coleridge

SLAG

Thief

Dad taught me to steal when I turned twelve.
In white apron over butcher's coat
hiked-up a foot to clear the sawdust floor,
pencil stub on trussing twine
dangling from a buttonhole,
boyhood snatched and left behind,
I was hammered into a counterman.
Smile, say 'Help you ma'am?',
give her odd weight
(even's too easy to calculate)
and add five percent to every sale,
or the Chains will eat our lunch.

Long ago I forgave his lies
that made me a thief so he could buy
a Jersey skiff, flash a two-inch roll,
and Mondays after *Schvitz* visit his trull.
But the customers don't pardon me:
should grandee, politician, fellow praise
service I've rendered, building raised,
once more across the counter shoppers stand
empty bags in outstretched hands,
Blondie, with her seven ragged kids,
baggers, dailies, handy-men,
discount coupons crumpled in their fists,
the working or redundant poor
I stole from weekly at his store,
stare, point, till I turn aside,
crimson, drop my eyes, and convert
laudation that should shrive me into dirt.

Primer

Mom slides two bucks
into the beat cop's palm
to ignore her Chevy
by the hydrant,
then goes to her weekly manicure.
Dad's sawbuck
buys the checker's wink
at the way-bill he should clock
for unbilled items,
like the hams chucked in our truck
along with our order on the loading dock.
Yeah, two-bit bribes,
but they knead and mould
the plastic mind of an eight-year-old.

Impostor Syndrome

An hour south of Wall Street,
past tulips, toddlers on swings,
cyclists, runners, Frisbees tossed
by girls in shimmering orange shorts,
I walk to the Institute library
to borrow the *Shorter OED*
laid by to welcome my stay.

A lay guest here before,
haunted by my familiar hissing
You have no business in this place,
today a librarian's courtesy, and spring,
muffle that devil at my ear
until it's almost impossible to hear
You're a wannabe from a trading floor.

Traitor

For even life in exile… is not as bad
as life alone in one's own country.
                    The World of Yesterday, Stefan Zweig

Two-ton eagle above the stairs,
soldiers cradling M16s,
flags everywhere,
the Consul's *Why?*,
the oath I swear
to *absolutely and entirely*
renounce my… nationality,
murmur *Traitor*, as I stand,
cancelled blue passport in hand,
a grey haired alien on foreign land.

Forty years doubts brewed in me
about Yankee Doodle verities
poured into us as kids,
corroded loyalty to hostility,
and left no choice at last but quit
the homeland I never fit.

I feel no remorse,
but wonder, nonetheless,
how Dreyfus felt, braced
on the square at *l'Ecole Militaire*,
sword snapped, disgraced,
reviled for what he did not do,
though faith, not fury, stood him askew.

Worship

My heroes have always been cowboys,
and still are, it seems...
> Willie Nelson

I idolised three simple men,
the seaman Holmes, the boxer Joe,
the hit-man Uncle Al, and from
their lives knocked up a creed
I lived by in the streets, a hymn
to seas' remorseless harmonies,
rage, and cold control.

To finish me took fifteen years,
a Grand Tour through four trades,
in six cities under three flags.
I fell in with thieves: double-
dipping bureaucrats, bent lawyers,
peacock generals in a libel case.
When these acid travels ended
my saints were slag, my brows knit,
and all my hymns re-writ.

Late Self Portrait

Venus fades; I stretch, rise,
shit, down pills, exercise,
blink till an image clarifies
that ego will not recognise –
sallow, ruptured, rag doll's guise,
melting jowls, pecs, gut, thighs –
and with hospice hope avert my eyes.

PRACTICE

Texaco Saturday Afternoon Opera

But this or such was Bleistein's way
T.S. Eliot, 'Burbank with a Baedeker:
Bleistein with a Cigar'

Talk sputters out, house lights lower,
a white wand rises with the scrim
and I see Chick not Lohengrin,
white coat and apron amid clutter,
salt beef, herrings, dills in brine,
rye bread piles three feet high
crusted with mountaineering flies,
stone streets outside his deli lined
with trash, graffiti walls and doors
where derelicts in newsprint quilts
doze like rank question marks on silt,
Cadillacs, pimps, and fat arsed whores:
childhood holograms that contain
lunch break sights when I worked with Dad.

Two decades on, a Yale law grad,
I've come back, first class, by plane
to survey all with widened eyes –
dying neighbourhood, dying shop,
anglicised surname a prop
above steel grates – unrecognised
until I interrupt the Jew
making sandwiches. *Danila?*
I puff up to launch my vita…

A radio warns curtain's due,
his welcome turns apology:
It's starting now, I've got to go,
the Met's doing 'Seraglio'.

The store goes dark, the patron keys
the lock and leaves me curb side, stunned,
complacencies of law courts undone
by an old shop keeper's passion.

Practice

We learned law was a calling
to build the new Jerusalem.
No one taught about the galleys
where this ancient craft is plied.
Up, back, down, pull,
up, back, down... *Keep your time*
in six-minute segments, a shit's
a billable event. What matters
is will it work and what's the risk.
Remember, rainmakers make partner.

You need not ship in law firms long
before your eyes burn reading briefs,
head throbs tracing labyrinthine codes
eighty hours a week,
and conscience daily coarsens
swinging between the tholes
of what's allowed and client wants,
as callus by callus you sweep into the dark.

Doktor Darker's Storage & Laundry

The window at his back cast him in shadow;
a Jugendstil desk kept visitors at bay.
He did not stand when I entered, or rose to go,
and sat silent, a grey patron at a tired play
listening to me invoke secrecy.
His raised palm cut me off: *Yung man,*
I don't care how your client makes money,
or who he is, but by law must ask two kvestions:
duss he sell arms, or deal drugs? Und I
don't care vhat the answer is. Numbered
accounts, bearer bonds, gold pried
from teeth perhaps, lie locked in vaults under
our feet, till need or death brings settlors or heirs
with claim cheques for the launderer upstairs.

Singing School, 2009

Greed, for lack of a better word,
is good… the essence of the evolutionary spirit.
Gordon Gekko, *Wall Street*

To start, we'll have champagne, quail eggs, paté
de campagne; next, line caught bass, jugged hare;
haricot verts, pommes Dauphinoise to share;
two espressos, dopio, one sorbet…
a City gent, lawyer in tow, ordering
lunch in a winter of wealth's discontent.
Dark Bloombergs, dealing rooms, silent
shops, signs shouting *Liquidation, Closing*
Down, play no rôle in his recitation:
So trades went south; the Fed had to save us;
shit happens. Just don't fuck with my bonus.
(Slap… slap… slap… the clap of palm and truncheon.)

The host inclines his head, and sidles to
his question, flicks crumbs at the caster
set like a pawn between them, cups an ear:
can he claw another *rock* or two
from deals he did that decked economies,
cash for a *Koons*, perhaps, he'll have to store?

This is the lyric of the jungle floor,
a hymn to labyrinthine strategies
conjuring Xanadus from acronyms,
testosterone, that goads the proud to fraud,
and concupiscence, robed like a bawd,
garrotting sympathy and tempting prison.

from *EVERY WRONG DIRECTION*

Hucksters

Arrogance is a foul disease. Like cancer, it blows no trumpet to announce its presence. Success breeds confidence that rots to hubris, the way colon cancer sprouts in an intestine and spreads through the peritoneal cavity till it kills you. By the time you realise you're infected, you've made the mistakes that will destroy you. Arrogance is the winner's cancer.

Higher education, and what came with it, were a giddy ride. Few think me *college material* in 1960, when the good offices of a high school teacher secure my place at a workingman's college in Philadelphia. Four years later I'm at Cambridge, five more and I graduate Yale Law School. Philadelphia's top law firm gives me a three months' signing bonus to choose them over competing firms.

In the summer of 1965, 18 months after a broken neck will likely leave me a permanent quadriplegic, I sail the Atlantic east to west with three other men on a 39-foot ketch. Four years later I sail it again, west to east, on a different 39-footer.

Imperceptibly, I begin to assume I'll win every fight, get whatever I desire. The one thing beyond my power to have, one woman's love, I never accept, and dwell on for the rest of my life. Superior, un-humbled, I show up 2 September 1969 for my first day as an associate at Morgan Lewis and Bockius, which we called ML&B.

Hucksters
The advent of the Nixon administration and my politics barred me from my job of choice, lawyer in the Treasury's Office of Tax Legislative Counsel. Runner-up was lawyering in a prominent corporate law firm until I found a suitable government job. Lawyering in a major firm you are a professional, I thought, like a doctor or a priest, a sea change from flogging pork loin ends in a butcher shop, and a big firm's saving grace.

I found New York cramped, dark, and hostile, working there as a summer associate. Too many people labour and live in too little space in Manhattan. Experiments with rats show penning them in small cages increases their hostility; NYC does the same to people. My hostility needed no enhancing on the Big Apple's packed pavements; I returned to Philadelphia, rather than Wall Street, after Yale.

Philadelphia's four or five top firms, with one exception, were peas in a pod: all had large corporate clients – manufacturers, banks, insurance, pharmaceutical, real estate developers, media, service businesses; had DC offices; had offered a *signing bonus*; had courted me. But only one featured in a film.

The Young Philadelphian portrays the rise of a working-class boy, (Paul Newman) in post-WWII Philadelphia. He specialises in a new field, tax law, at the city's most prestigious law firm, makes partner, humbles the Main Line's *pezzonovante* (big shots), and wins the *great shiska*. I read the book, saw the movie, and knew ML&B was the model for the tale's 24-carat WASP law firm. Could I have gone anywhere else? I did not go to ML&B for their bonus, large DC office, or Republican political connections; I went because I dreamed it was my story.

ML&B, founded in 1873, looked the part of a leading *white shoe* law firm, outside and in. It sprawled across high floors of a half block square, 20-some storey grey granite building on the south-east corner of Broad Street and Sansom Street, a few blocks south of William Penn's hat. The building's 12-foot high bronze bound doors were so heavy that when the wind blew hard from the west in winter a man had to use both hands to pry them open. The elevators debouched onto the firm's nineteenth-floor reception lobby, walnut panelled, thickly carpeted. A walnut desk the size of a block from the base of Cheops' pyramid confronted arrivals. From behind this fortification a prim, thin, fiftyish receptionist, skirt three-inch below her knees, cleared visitors into the walnut-panelled waiting room to her right, or chirped *Good morning* to the senior partners as they strode to their offices down the walnut-panelled corridor to her left, where sombre portraits of the firm's founders stared sternly down at them. She smelled of attar of roses, the walnut panelling of lemon-oil furniture polish with which cleaners stroked it daily at dawn. Morgan Lewis' offices smelled of old money, and looked like a walnut lumber yard.

On the north-west corner opposite preened the Union League, a *Deuxième Empire* style, rusticated, brownstone and brick Civil War mansion. Founded in 1862, the Union League was the city's most exclusive private social club, the in-town watering hole for male *Black Book*[1] listees; neither women, Jews, blacks, *nouveaux riches* nor *arrivistes* were welcome as members or diners. My maternal grandfather, then a corrupt member of the Pennsylvania state legislature, was refused entry for lunch as a member's guest in the '40s. When I joined ML&B the *League* had been their lawyers' club of choice for 96 years.

Partners, and most associates, lived on the Main Line, in townships like Merion, Bryn Mawr, Radnor, Villanova, Devon, where Philadelphia's upper crust had lived and been rich together for more than a century. They summered in Northeast Harbor (sic) Maine, yachted, fox hunted, played tennis, golfed, and held debutante balls in their *restricted* country clubs. Female issue *prepped* at Holton Arms and The Baldwin School, male at Choate and Andover; the young ladies went on to Vassar and Smith, the young men to Princeton and Yale.

Associates joined ML&B straight from law school, became partners, and never left. The firm had counseled many of their clients for decades, some almost from its founding. Until the mid '60s, clients rarely had large *in-house* legal departments and, even rarer, substantial *in-house* tax groups. ML&B did all of some big corporates' legal work, and major clients paid them an annual retainer to be on call, whether they used them or not. Partners served on clients' boards as directors, and sometimes left to become their senior executives. These hoary, intertwined relationships, the retainers, relatively low overheads, the firm's ethos, stable partnership and reputation freed it to advise honestly, unconcerned whether its advice would lead to more business, or protect a relationship.

There was no policy that associates bill a minimum number of hours a year when I joined the firm. Eighty-hour work weeks were neither routine nor encouraged. ML&B had not tried to grow by hiring *laterals*, partners from other firms with portable *books* of

---

1 The Black Book is the US social register, in the 1960s with some 35,000 names of the bluest of blood.

business. The Bar Association forbade lawyers to advertise; the firm deemed it unseemly to shill for clients, or hustle work. Male lawyers were gentlemen, the few women lawyers ladies; all were counselors, not *service providers*. Practicing law at ML&B had long been an honourable profession, rather than a hustle, when I rounded the receptionist's desk to my first day at work, but the tectonic plates beneath corporate law practice had shifted, commercialisation had begun, and in their wake abasement to a service business followed.

ML&B's tax department was nine strong in 1969, five partners, four associates; in law firm argot it was *top-heavy*. The three senior partners were gentile gentlemen, with long established, secure practices: Tom Lefevre, the department's head and a specialist in reorganisations; Al McDowell, an expert in controversies – civil and criminal tax audits, investigations and litigation; H Peter Somers, an estate and gift tax guru who handled the tax and other affairs of the Campbell Soup heirs. They were counsellors, and prized as such by clients. But Tom and Al would soon retire, H Peter was mid-50s and absorbed in his practice. They were the past. *Top-heavy* firms of gentile gentlemen would not survive in the emerging world of corporate law practice; the status quo was not an option.

The remaining two partners were the Odell brothers, Stuart and Herb. Both were Jews, under 40, and not to the manor born. (ML&B kept its Jews in the tax department 50 years ago.) Neither had attended prestigious colleges or law schools, but did well at the nation's best graduate tax programmes. Stuart had been top of his LLM tax class at NYU, specialised in partnerships, equipment leasing, and tax shelters, and was a nationally acknowledged expert in all three. Herb was a litigator; and smoked cigars.

Their practices were transactional, either in newly-developed areas of tax law (Stuart's), or tax controversies (Herb's); both less secure than the senior partners' practices. Retainers in Stuart's area were rare and vanishing; in Herb's, illogical. Both had to scurry for new business and were better equipped for it than their seniors. Stuart succeeded Tom Lefevre as head of the tax department, before he was lured to a New York firm. Herb remained behind.

Partners as well as associates were on deck well before nine, Mondays through Fridays. Most associates worked a half day Saturday, as often did the Odells, and not infrequently senior partners. Associates vied to bill the most hours… and be seen to.

No one at ML&B had mentioned billable hours when I interviewed. There was no minimum billable requirement until sometime after I left; but there might as well have been. Within days of starting work, I gleaned from associates that partners *hoped* we would bill a minimum of 1800 hours a year. *Less is more* was not a rubric applied to billing.

To bill an honest 35-40 hours a week (1800÷49 weeks) meant spending 55-60 hours in the office in those pre-computer days. The pressure to bill more was palpable, and increasing. We understood copious billings greased the rails to partnership, and weighed heavily in deliberations on your annual bonus. No junior kept *banker's hours* at ML&B.

Minimum billable requirements, formal or not, are un-professional. It assumes, wrongly, there is always adequate work to be done. Suppose not; do you spin out what you do have; cheat? If you're faster than others, spot an answer quickly by chance or ability, should you be penalised, or the client denied the benefit? If a partner responsible for feeding you work doesn't, should you be faulted? Is every minute spent thinking about a client billable; is taking a shit a billable event? I understood overheads, that associates were well paid, partners had to pay school fees and club dues, hence billing was important. But I expected emphasis to be on advising well first, and billing second, not the other way round. Billable requirements are unsurprising in service businesses like accounting and management consulting. I hadn't expected, or been led to expect them at ML&B.

I must have heard the phrase *rainmaker* before I lowered myself into the standard issue swivel chair behind my desk at ML&B, perhaps during my previous summer's stint on Wall Street, but it did not come readily to mind. A few hours later, David O'Brien, a civillised, decent, corporate law partner just over 50, assigned to be my mentor and familiarise me with the firm, introduced me to Bill Goldstein. As we left Goldstein's office, David told me he had come from a policy-making decision at the Treasury, was well regarded in the firm, and especially prized as a *rainmaker. What's a rainmaker? A lawyer good at getting new clients or work.* Lawyers and accountants use the term routinely. I've not heard it applied to other professionals, like GPs, surgeons, architects, or academics.

Not only partners were supposed to make rain. Associates were urged to write trade articles, entertain likely clients, socialise with them in the right clubs. We saw the firm's heroes were *rainmaking* partners and heard they got the largest shares of the partnership pie. We watched associates quickly become partners if they brought in business. So, we chased possible new business ourselves. Client snaffling was another topic that lay doggo when I interviewed.

Shortly after I joined the firm, another associate rushed up to me as I was leaving one evening and thrust a tabloid in my hand. *You've GOT to see this.* It was a trade journal whose front page bannered *Top 20 Law Firms' Profits.* Inside were listed the leading 20 firms by billings, profits and per partner income; ML&B was there. His almost breathless prurient interest was unsurprising; the firms' two legal castes, partners and associates, were fixated on how much their peers made, a fixation ubiquitous at the big law firms. An image from boyhood trips to *schvitz* popped into my mind: my father and two other ghetto butchers wrapped in sheets and towels, only their eyes, noses and mouths bare, reclining on deck chairs *schvitzing* (sweating) after a *platza* and exaggerating to each other how much they made.

With client getting and money the measure of men, envy was rife at ML&B. Status fixed by salary and bonus, or share of partnership profits, discouraged friendship, camaraderie and mutual assistance. Jealousy and envy burbled just below the firm's surface; occasionally it boiled over.

William A Macan IV, WAM IV as he initialed memos, laboured in the office next to mine. He was 30, a Penn law grad, married with one child, and lived on the Main Line. Like the younger tax partners and associates, excepting me, he came accredited to ML&B, with an LLM in taxation and clerkship on the US Tax Court. He understudied Stuart Odell on leveraged leasing deals, which were often tax shelters, and a *hot* area of tax practice. To be a partner was his grail, a common quest among associates.

WAM IV was a florid, barrel-bellied man who appeared always to be hurrying, his breastbone thrust forward like a snow plough's blade, or fast strutting like a turkey avoiding danger, or Mussolini leading his *Fascisti.* He looked half again older than he was, a look he cultivated. He had a temper, and deployed it against juniors and staff. We shared a young Italian-American secretary whose skills needed burnishing. More than once he reduced her to tears after she mangled a draft. Angered, which he often was, he flushed British pillar box red. Superiors he flattered, juniors ignored, disdained my paltry tax expertise and me, and refused to help me the one time I asked. ML&B made him a partner in due course, after which he jumped ship for the New York office of a London firm.

We started at ML&B the same day. Even with our office doors shut, which mine rarely was, we could hear the other's phone ring through our common wall. Cambridge supervisions had taught me if I couldn't explain a problem and solution so a layman could understand it, I didn't understand it myself. So I strove to simplify tax issues as much as possible; clients welcomed the effort. Years in the butcher shop may also have helped me discuss tax with clients because they gave me a good grounding in business, and corporate taxation is all about business. (It can be understood as, essentially, the answers to three questions: *Have you made a profit? If so, how much do you owe Uncle Sam? Can you avoid that debt without doing time?*) Perhaps, as some said, clients found me intelligible because I oversimplified, being a tax neophyte lacking, say, WAM IV's specialised knowledge, and inappreciative of the subtleties of a problem. Or perhaps they just appreciated my predilection to say bluntly what I thought they should do, and opine on their chances of success if they did it. (I'm often wrong, but never in doubt.) For any or all these reasons, or because I was a colourful cuckoo in a nest of subfusc suits, clients often called for advice.

One afternoon, after a morning when my phone had rung incessantly, WAM IV stormed into my office, slammed the door behind him and screamed *Why does your phone ring all the time!* He knew the answer. *Well, clients call me. Don't they call you?* He slammed the door again on the way out. That my ringing phone drove WAM IV mad on the other side of the wall caused me no undue regret.

Shortly after 10 one morning we were all summoned to an emergency meeting in Tom Lefevre's corner office. The chief executive of the firm's largest client had just called to say he had won a new car in a charity raffle the night before, and the value of the car, which was taxable income to him, would push him into a higher tax bracket, and cost him more than the car was worth. What should he do?

Our nine-man tax department scrambled *en masse* for the answer. The search was fraught; would we find an acceptable solution PDQ? Within an hour we had it: refuse to accept the car. At today's billing rates that blitz cost either the CEO or his employer $7,000 (£4,500), assuming it was billed, or the firm if it was written off as *PD* (practice development), the euphemism for wining, dining, and generally pandering to clients. The taxpayer was the CEO, not the company, and the amount at issue could not have been great. The panic to satisfy him demonstrated his power to take the public company's business elsewhere, and the partners' slavish fears that if in the least dissatisfied, he might. Peers and partners dwelled in anxiety about whether clients might move to another law firm. In the case of the largest clients, anxiety rose to hysteria.

Most mornings around 11 a.m., a bent old man shuffled through the tax department towards the corner offices where the senior partners sat. Perhaps 25 minutes later he passed by again on his way to the elevator bank. His hands were stained, as was the apron he wore over work shirt and pants. In his left hand he lugged a worn shoeshine box.

I never learned his name, or anything about him, though think he was Italian. He crept from office to office offering to shine the lawyers' shoes. Some regularly accepted. Herb Odell and I were discussing a problem he'd assigned me when the shoeshine man appeared in the doorway. Herb crooked his finger to motion him in, swivelled his chair, swung his legs from under to the side of his desk, and received brush and polish from the old man at his feet without pausing our conversation, or dousing his cigar.

Shoeshine men on their knees at a partner's feet were a common tableau in big firm law offices. One made the rounds at the Wall Street firm where I'd worked the summer before. Associates often aped their betters and had the shoeshine man spiff up their shoes as well; I was not among them.

ML&B was not unique; what it was becoming, the other big firms were too. America's '60s economy powered changes that ineluctably sapped the professional foundations of big firm law practice. By the mid to late '70s corporate law practice was fully commercialised, a service business, not profession. Six engines, economic and social, torpedoed traditional firms – the growth of in-house law departments, fee pressure, death of the retainer, plethora of new laws and regulations, rise of the accountants, and distrust of outside counsel. The first three led to lower billings at old line firms, the second trio to competition from new. The net effect was to sink firms that couldn't adapt.

Today, 49 years after I worked there, ML&B is the world's ninth largest law firm, with two thousand lawyers in 30 offices around the world generating $2 billion p.a. in revenue, rather than the perhaps 150 lawyers in two offices it was in my day. ML&B survived through decades that saw many traditional firms fade, die, be absorbed or go bankrupt. It prospered by cutting costs, hiring laterals, opening new offices in far-flung cities and countries, acquiring other firms, absorbing them, or raiding their best practices, as well as growing organically. It now is a complex international service business, not a professional law practice, its practitioners *service providers* with revenue generation (partners) or billable hour (associates) targets to meet.

No light[1] sculpture scrolled *SNOOKERED* on a column of bright orange lights on the wall behind the receptionist's redoubt. I realised only gradually, over weeks and months, I'd become a piece-worker like my grandmother, my garments memoranda and opinions instead of frilly ladies' blouses, and a huckster once again. Lured with attar of roses and walnut-panelled walls, with 96 years' honourable history and distinguished reputation, with gentile gentlemen like Tom Lefevre, Al McDowell and H Peter Somers, I'd been had. Beneath fine woods, prim receptionists and white Van Heusen shirts was simply another service business chasing customers and sales. The firm had not deliberately deceived me; like all the big firms market pressures were forcing it to commercialise, perhaps insensibly to its seniors. Nevertheless, I felt baited and switched, like the wife who believes she's wed a paragon and in days discovers he's a cheat. Disillusioned and angry, my anger and arrogance showed.

I flaunted my contempt for ML&B in ways small and large. Back in Philly, I rented a flat in a very slowly gentrifying south centre city area a few blocks from where I'd been born. My birth block was

---

1 See Jenny Holzer.

unreconstructed slum, a street too far south for gentrification. No ML&B lawyer lived near me, and I wore my inner-city digs as a badge of egalitarian superiority,[1] neglecting to mention when my flat was broken into and stripped of all worth taking within a month of moving in.

With several non-firm lawyers I opened a free legal clinic to represent poor tenants in fights with slumlords. I held its organisational meeting in ML&B's main conference room so my somewhat scuzzy *pro bono* co-counsels might shock my uptown peers.[2] The clinic generated squeals of outrage from sued landlords, and favourable stories in the city's press. ML&B's seniors were not amused by the publicity, or the clinic's anti-capitalist slant.

Shortly after I'd been shown the article on big firm partners' profits, my mentor, David O'Brien called me to his office to ask how I was getting on. He knew that private practice had been my second choice, had seen the pro bono lawyers file into the conference room, that I lived far from the Main Line and did not attend the first several firm functions, so could not have been surprised when I blurted out *Dave, we're not practicing law. All we're doing is selling pork chops.*

Italian immigrant tailors in South Philadelphia advertised in the local papers, an ad of theirs caught my eye, and I decided to have a three-piece suit made for the office. The wool suiting was a light denim blue with wide, bold, purple-red stripes, like material for a baseball team's uniform. Firm gossip soon dubbed it the *baseball suit*. The receptionist's eyes widened, the corners of her mouth drooped into frown the first morning I passed her kitted out in it. Its broad coloured stripes, too light for business blue field, and tight waistcoat gave it a '30s gangsterish air. It did not give of wealth or pomp, like nothing else at ML&B. The *baseball suit* spat *Fuck you!* to everyone at the firm, lawyers and secretaries alike. I retired it from service when I left ML&B.

WAM IV, and I in the *baseball suit*, were waiting for the elevator one lunch time. As the elevator doors parted on a car packed with partners including Mr MacIntosh, the firm's Managing Partner,

---

1   See *Uptown Girl*, Billy Joel
2   op.cit.

he whispered, *Please, don't say anything to me while we're in the elevator.* I turned to WAM IV as the car began its 19-floor drop and said in a raised, clear voice, *Bill, what do you think about squirrels?* Heads swivelled, alarm appeared on a few faces, Mr MacIntosh ostentatiously looked away. WAM IV turned boiled-lobster red and, except in tax meetings, never spoke to me again.

Tax season, the four months before corporate, when individual US tax returns are due, runs from January to April 15th. Partners were often in the office on Saturdays from February on, helping answer the flood of questions that arise while returns are prepared. My office was first on the left as you entered the tax department, so I could see whomever came in. Snow was threatening on a late February Saturday morning around 10 a.m. when Tom Lefevre passed by my office with a copy of *I And Thou* tucked under his arm; Buber's book of moral philosophy was on the bestseller list at the time. Tom said *Good morning* as he passed. Instead of a greeting, I blurted *What are you doing with that book?* Tom paused, turned, stared at me for several seconds, then said *I read too, Dan,* and walked on.

A few minutes later I knocked on his office door, entered at his *Come in,* and apologised. He raised his eyes, fixed me with a doleful stare, lowered them again to the Tax Court Reporter open on his desk and motioned me from the room. The dried sweat smell of shame still wreathes me, 48 years later.

Familiars

I strode down the Hill's four flights
to wife and victory dinner,
a green Treasury lawyer
who'd convinced the Senate Leader
to spike a sulphur miner's loophole.

Their lobbyist phoned at eight;
no hello, no good morning:
Y'all did that, didn't you,
you little son-of-a-bitch?
Well son, in thirty minutes
you're gonna change your mind.
Click. Within the hour
my boss stood at the door,
weight on one leg, then the other:
The Chairman called. I'm sorry, but…
you know, he's from their state.
If mining's out,
he'll kill the bill.
So, well… you understand…

Sure, I knew the score
and long ago was wise
to family who were fixers,
bent cops, racketeers.
Still, I was surprised;
none of my kin wore coats and ties.

Heeps

Agents, never principals,
they sell themselves by the hour
seven days a week
to audit, parse laws, advise,
dwell in faux-colonial mansions
and summer cottages seaside,
cradle low seven figure wealth
in Treasuries, large caps,
and only pick low-hanging fruit.

Yet at night's fag end
neurons coded in the Pleistocene
to flee shadows of substantial things
fire at the creaking of a gate,
hail pummelling roof slate,
a squirrel scuttling under the eaves
and fling these over-prudent men
from tangled, sweat-soaked sheets,
short-breathed, groping for inhalers,
though no drug can ease their breathing,
nor title, nor everything they own.

Sum

I dropped my drawers in the globe's bazaars,
New York, London, Al Khobar,
'Cisco, DC, Zug, Tehran
as lawyer, banker, businessman
for hordes of exotic deals:
arms, roads, airports, hospitals,
gas turbines for the dead Shah's fields,
tax dodges to fatten yields.
My wages were a sceptic eye
that probes lover, friend, passer-by
for greed, envy, ego, pride
at the root of even noble acts: a curse,
to rummage the best for the worst.

from *EVERY WRONG DIRECTION*

Knaves

I believe in America, Amerigo Bonasera tells Don Corleone as he pleads *for justice* in *The Godfather*'s first frame. Growing up, I heard something like it from my father; it's something I might have said my first day as a lawyer for Treasury's International Tax Counsel (ITC). The Don gives the undertaker *justice* in exchange for the fealty he swears. I gave justice to no one during my 18 months at Treasury and did not believe in America when I left.

A year earlier, ML&B had rewarded me well at bonus time, despite my contemptuous behaviour. Clients continued to call for advice, my billables were healthy. But everyone at ML&B knew I was incorrigibly unclubbable, and no matter how much rain I made, or hours billed, would never make partner. They also knew I wanted a job at Treasury, not a partnership. A few months later they corralled it for me.

At a weekly ML&B tax department meeting soon after I started, Tom Lefevre asked for a volunteer to specialise in the Internal Revenue Code's (Code) foreign sections. When no one else volunteered, I raised my hand. Two years at Cambridge had made me less provincial, and convinced that business' future was global. If business was going global, international tax lawyers had a future.

The foreign sections overlay three non-tax concepts on the Code's economic and accounting foundation – jurisdiction,[1] anti-avoidance,[2] bi-lateral tax treaties.[3] These sections do not redefine income and expense for a foreign context, rather they allocate them between

---

1 Secs. 861–864 source of income and expense rules.
2 Secs. 951-954;
3 [118] treaties with other countries to avoid double taxation of the same item of income.

jurisdictions, and attempt to prevent offshore tax avoidance. Most US tax lawyers shied from learning the foreign sections. The few who didn't formed a small, close knit Acela Express[1] coterie.

Stan Weiss was one of their brotherhood. A partner in ML&B's DC office, he had worked in international tax at Treasury, and with me my first year at the firm. Stan heard of an opening at ITC, asked me if I was interested, and recommended me for it. ML&B seconded his recommendation. I interviewed with Bob Cole, the ITC, in mid-February 1971. A few weeks later Cole offered me an attorney-advisor slot on his staff, to begin in June after a routine FBI background check. We pledged some of my wealthy second wife's stock to buy a three-storey, four-bedroom, brown brick townhouse at 34th and P streets in Georgetown, and prepared to process to Washington.

The FBI flunked me, and Cole withdrew his offer; I'd been hired and fired in six weeks without working a day. I appealed to ML&B for help, reasoning that if I didn't get the post it would reflect worse on them than me; when word got out clients might want to know what kind of associates they were hiring who couldn't pass a routine FBI check. The firm made inquiries and discovered it was my *pro bono* work for poor tenants that scuppered me, not traces of my misspent youth; representing poor people was politically incorrect. Mr MacIntosh, ML&B's managing partner, called his friend Hugh Scott, US Senator from Pennsylvania and Republican Senate Minority Leader, and a few days later Cole renewed his offer.

Nixon by then had been in office two years, and my experience at the sharp point of his right-wing government did not augur well. I should have thought carefully before accepting Cole's offer a second time. But we already owned a fancy Georgetown house, and I was 29 years old and indestructible.

At 7:30 a.m. on a warm morning in late June 1971, I head my bike down M Street in Georgetown toward Main Treasury, a grand,

---

1 The Acela Express is a fast Amtrak train that runs between DC and NYC, and is popular with executives travelling frequently between the two power centres.

whited sepulchre at 15th and Pennsylvania Ave. This Greek revival building fronting Pennsylvania Ave., with a 350-foot north façade, Ionic columned portico, and White House next door is familiar to anyone who's looked at the back of a $10 bill. Pedalling past the White House fence toward Treasury's underground garage, I grow a tad taller, my voice deepens, and I'm Rick Blaine, pistol in hand, about to tell Captain Renault: *Not so fast, Louis*.[1]

I report to Cole's 3rd floor office suite, and a secretary shows me five doors north up a hushed, high-ceilinged corridor to mine. To the south from my office window I can just see the Washington Monument on the Mall. Cole comes in an hour later, welcomes me, and hands me my first project: analyze a draft *private member's* bill to bail out some mining companies, and tell the Assistant Secretary whether Treasury should support it.

The US Constitution's *origination* clause says *All bills for raising Revenue shall originate in the House of Representatives...* Even Presidents must use a friendly Congresswoman to introduce tax legislation they want. Not infrequently large corporates avail themselves of this rule, and have their congressman or woman introduce a *private member's* bill to fix their tax problems.

In that summer of 1971 Anaconda Copper, Kennecott Copper, and Cerro (AKC) had one they needed fixed. A few weeks earlier Salvador Allende, democratically elected Marxist President of Chile, completed the nationalisation (expropriation if you like) of AKC's copper mines. They received nothing in return. General Augusto Pinochet led a US sponsored military coup a few years later that toppled Allende, who committed suicide. But in 1971 Allende sat tall in the saddle, and inflicted a collective $80 million capital loss on AKC, ($500 million in 2018 dollars). The copper companies realised no tax benefit from the loss of their mines; the Code only allowed them to take their losses against capital gains, and not unusually they had none. Now they wanted Congress to allow them to deduct these losses from their ordinary income, which would have given them a roughly $40 million tax benefit (a quarter billion in 2018 dollars) and halved their losses.

---

1   1942 movie, *Casablanca*.

The Code's treatment of AKC's capital gains and losses was symmetrical and fair. Had AKC had a $500 million capital gain, it would have been taxed at the much lower 15 percent capital gain rate, rather than the 48 percent ordinary income rate. AKC wanted it both ways – plusses taxed at the lowest rate, minuses allowed at the highest. The *private member's* bill I was to analyze was their begging bowl.

I detailed in a memo why the law change AKC wanted was a Treasury raid, and recommended we oppose their bill, which would kill it. A *private member's* bill that goes to the Hill without Treasury's imprimatur is DOA, dead on arrival. Wednesday at day's end I sent the memo to the Assistant Secretary's office, and next day Jack Nolan, Deputy Assistant Secretary for Tax Policy, asked me to meet him at 10 a.m. on Saturday morning to discuss it.

The offices of high ranking Treasury officials' are large and imposing; Nolan's no exception. He sat behind a seven-foot-long, three-foot-wide mahogany desk awash in papers. The tax world regarded Nolan as the real Assistant Tax Secretary, and his putative boss, Edwin S. Cohen, Assistant Secretary for Tax, no more than the Administration's front man. Nolan was in his late 50s, slightly above middle height, balding, colourless, formal, and efficient. He had been a senior, highly regarded tax partner at Miller and Chevalier, DC's pre-eminent white shoe tax firm, and was the most powerful tax official in the Treasury.

He began by thanking me for meeting on a Saturday morning, then larded praise on my memo. He picked it from the paper heap before him, read conclusions and recommendation aloud, then said *I agree. We'll oppose the bill.* I'd stopped a theft; baulked the forces of evil; was Rick Blaine. Adrenalin whipped through me, and I thought *so this is what power feels like.* I'd been given morphine injections for months, aged 21, to quell pain from a broken neck; this felt better.

I rose, was half turned to the door, when Nolan said *Is there anything we can do for them?*

We? Should Treasury warp the Code to subsidise behemoth mining companies? The glow Nolan's compliments and concurrence kindled faded, Mittyish haze evaporated, reality flooded back; once again I was standing on the Tabriz before his desk. This was Nixon's first term Republican administration, enraged that a Marxist had won a fair election in America's backyard, confronted with a plea for help from American miners who'd had *their* copper stolen by a *commie*; what did I expect?

A way to appease Nolan and still thwart the copper companies came to mind; I answered: *Maybe they could get a ruling.* IRS will rule on matters of law at a taxpayer's request if the question involves a tax principle of general interest. It will not rule on facts, or mixed fact and law questions, like whether AKC's stock in their nationalised foreign subsidiaries was wholly worthless; normally does not initiate a ruling but waits for a taxpayer to request it; and will not alter standing interpretations of law to accommodate a taxpayer. The Service has complete discretion to rule or not, for or against the taxpayer.

To rule that Chile's nationalisations entitled AKC to an ordinary loss would require the Service to investigate facts surrounding the takings, and expand existing law in AKC's favour. I thought it would be an arctic day in hell before they did either, which was why AKC had come knocking on Treasury's door begging for a statutory change.

But Nolan seemed pleased, which should have worried me. I assumed the ruling idea appealed because it was sufficiently plausible to fob off the miners. A more experienced, humbler Treasury lawyer would have reflected that Nolan was an old Washington hand who'd forgotten more about applicable law, rulings and how the IRS worked than this 29-year-old Washington ingénue before him would ever learn. But I was young and snotty, no use to talk to me.

Nolan and three AKC representatives were in the Secretary's grand third floor conference room when I entered two days later on Monday morning at 11 a.m. The three older men were chatting familiarly. A man my age, clearly the miners' *bag carrier*, stood two steps outside the clot of elders and their conversation. Five people meeting in so large a room – nearly a tractor trailer long, and one and half times the width of one – was incongruous, and injected a lugubrious note. A meeting in Nolan's office conference room would have been more comfortable, but Nolan presumably wanted to impress the AKC reps that Treasury took their problem seriously.

The older men were Ray Sherfy, Fred Peel and Nolan. Sherfy was chief lobbyist for the American Mining Congress, and brother to Larry Sherfy, one of Jack Nolan's ex-law partners at Miller and Chevalier. Peel had written the four-volume bible on consolidated corporate tax returns, and was also an ex-partner of Nolan's at M&C. The gathering was more cousin's club than business meeting.

Nolan introduced me to Sherfy and Peel. Sherfy introduced me to the *bag carrier*, and we all sat down at the 25-foot-long conference table: Nolan at its head, Sherfy at his left hand, Peel next to Sherfy, and the *bag carrier* next to Peel. I sat, ignored, on Nolan's right some way down the table, within earshot to hear and take notes, but not participate in the conversation.

Nolan spoke first. *Ray, Treasury will not support your bill.* The suppliants' faces dropped in tandem, like the gartered legs of a chorus line. Sherfy began to argue, Nolan cut him off. *I'm sorry, Ray, but the Administration cannot support legislation to help you out.*

Jack, is thar anythin yuh kin do fur us?

Well, we think you might be able to get a ruling.

Jack, rulin's take a long time, and we need help quick.

Nolan swivelled right, looked down the table at me and said *Dan, how long do you think it will take us to get a ruling for them?* The others' heads snapped left from Jack to me, but they were too far away to notice my flush. *US get a ruling for THEM?* Surely Treasury didn't procure rulings, taxpayers did that. It hadn't occurred to me Treasury would run interference for the mining companies with the Service, heavy it, put Treasury's ponderous finger on the scale, do covertly what it refused to do openly. It seemed the Nixon Administration did not object to bailing out the miners, so long as it was done without the public noticing.

We rose, and Ray Sherfy hurried down and around the long conference table to shake my hand. He gripped it less perfunctorily than at our introduction 15 minutes earlier, held it for a moment or two, clutched my elbow with his left hand, pulled me a little closer and said *What was yawh name again, young man.*

Dan Burt.

Waal, wuh'll have lots to talk about tuh get this rollin'. Y'all free for lunch tuhmorrah? I had a new best friend.

On the corner of 18th and K Streets, the heart of the lobbyist gold coast, stood the marquee of the Maison Blanche, the Capital's premier French restaurant. I arrived there on time at 12.15 next day, sweaty from the heat of the sun after a seven-minute pedal from Treasury, chained my bike to one of two thin, steel, curbside poles supporting the marquee, and entered. Mine was the only bike in sight.

Ray, Fred and the *bag carrier* were waiting. The restaurant was not quite wine cellar cool, panelled in dark wood, with a burgundy red, thick nap wool carpet. The ceiling was high, perhaps 12 foot, the tables sufficiently far apart, the carpets absorptive so that it was easy to hear your dining partners, but difficult to hear another table's conversation. There were no food smells. This was ground zero of the three martini lunch.

Jean-Pierre, the owner, greeted me like a relative. Clearly he'd been told to look out for me, and certainly knew *Monsieur Sherfy*. He showed me to an ample, round table in the right rear corner of the dining room farthest from the entrance, the most private spot in the restaurant. I shook hands with my hosts and settled down to my first, long, boozy lobbyist's lunch.

Surely Treasury rules forbade staff accepting expensive lunches of the sort I was about to have, but no one at Treasury had told me about them, and I would have ignored them in any case. A lifetime's dinners at *Le Tour d'Argent* could not have suborned me to help my hosts obtain their ruling, nor curb my plans to scuttle it. But the Maison Blanche's Camparis, *canard a l'orange*, '59 clarets, maroon plush chairs and sparkling linens, the irony of being feted by people I was trying to screw, added a spy's piquancy to this and frequent future lunches.

That first lunch lasted until the staff began discreetly trying to prepare the tables around us for the dinner sitting. I remember my two double Camparis, my aperitif of choice at the time, our two bottles of claret, *coupes aux marrons*, my first experience of the dessert and a favourite ever since, port, and a superb blacklisted Havana cigar, but no appetiser or entrée. I remember Sherfy leaning towards me as soon as I was seated and saying, *Yuh shur look young. We thought yuh were a summer intern when we first saw yuh.* A little later he told me how bright my future was, how keen the big DC law firms would be to hire me, especially if the Mining Congress recommended me. The contrapositive, how bleak my way would be if I disappointed the miners, went unsaid. I left in a haze of bonhomie, wobbled my way back to Treasury, and slept at my desk till almost quitting time two hours later.

But business had been done, between the bouquets and the port. AKC were to draft and submit a ruling request to IRS' Branch 5, the foreign section specialists, within two weeks. A blind copy would be sent to me, and after a few days I'd call the Branch's head so he was aware of Treasury's interest and desire to expedite the request. I'd bird dog the ruling thereafter until the Service issued it.

Following that lunch until just before Christmas, I delayed, dissembled, leaked and undercut the ruling's progress every way I could. Treasury sent a letter to the IRS Commissioner supporting AKC's request a day after IRS received it. I met with Branch 5's boss, Ed Goldwag, a looming, gentle, six-foot-plus career civil servant, gave him an unvarnished history of the ruling request's provenance, and promised to help derail it. Branch 5 opposed issuing the ruling after they studied the request, and dragged its feet.

A Treasury economist, Marcia Field, introduced me to her husband Tom, who published *Tax Analysts and Advocates*, a fledgling, muck-raking journal for tax specialists dedicated to giving an unvarnished, generally left leaning, reformist account of tax news. I told Tom in detail about the AKC ruling request, and he printed a piece critical of what was happening. But the mainstream press didn't pick the issue up.

Branch 5 dug its heels in deeper. I defended them when Nolan complained about how long the ruling was taking, and continued enjoying long, sybaritic lunches at the Maison Blanche on the Mining Congress' tab, sometimes with Sherfy and *the bag carrier*, or, more frequently as the process dawdled on, *the bag carrier* alone. Invitations to Maison Blanche lunches dwindled as Indian summer turned to proper autumn and the ruling remained bogged down; they stopped completely when the trees were nearly bare and there was still no ruling.

Nolan's frustration mounted. He was scheduled to end his two-year stint at Treasury early in the new year, and return through the revolving door to Miller & Chevalier, where he and his partners would profit from his knowledge gained, enhanced reputation, and contacts made or improved during his Treasury sojourn. In November, Secretary of the Treasury, John Connally, former Texas governor and passenger in the front seat of the limousine with Kennedy in Dallas eight years earlier, who had taken a bullet as well, wrote to the Commissioner about the ruling to the effect of *Get this done!* In late December 1971, the Service published Revenue Ruling 1972–71, the first ruling of the coming year, giving the miners what they asked for. The reward for my quixotic labours was a jaundiced view of the American way of making law, my first experience of fine clarets and burgundies, and a penchant for *coupes aux marrons.*

Gold Rush

i. *Arrivals Hall, Jeddah, 1976*

Wool suit and cotton kameez
jostle on luggage mountains
for their Samsonites, Louis Vuittons,
string-bound cardboard cartons,
like rag-pickers on a dump.
At their feet, russet fellahin
from the Horn, or huts in Yemen,
bare-toed in sandals and soiled thobes,
add to the piles from L-1011s.
In the scrum, six centuries elide;
Huntsman and hajji,
Bell Labs and prayer rug collide.

ii. *Prospecting*

Chancers swarmed over Saudi
like locusts across oases,
chasing deals and RFPs
the *Oil Shock* shook loose.
Lured from armchairs in Pall Mall,
Parisian *grands hôtels*,
steak houses in Houston,
bordellos in Beirut,
they stalk contracts with kick-backs
masquerading as commissions
to conniving Saudi agents.
No road is laid, no school raised,
no tank clanks off a Ro-Ro
a middleman has not greased.

iii. *Site Work*

Yellow Komatsu backhoes
rip chunks from mud-brick walls;
pneumatic drills chew stones
pre-Islamic masons spalled;
swarms of Toyota pick-ups
swallow rebars spewed from ships.
Hydro-carbon hunger
unleashed these beasts
that remorselessly devour
Jeddah's ancient streets.

iv. *Departure*

Petro-dollars cycling round
like suds in a washing machine
bought airports, fighters, microwave towers,
the ephemera of states,
and parvenu trappings like Rolexes, Ferraris,
tight-assed blondes and boys.

Red Sea to Gulf of Aden
steel and glass spindles rose,
macadam strapped the Kingdom,
then oil prices froze
and the black-gold *dabkeh* stopped.

Bulldozers rusted, cranes dropped,
con men and contractors decamped
and abandoned their slurs
scrawled on compound walls,
sand-niggers, towel-heads;
left the curtain-wall towers
that guest workers would run;
and disowned the generation of dragons' teeth
that sprouted believers
with Kalashnikovs and RPGs
who stormed the *Masjid al-Haram*,
in the late November sun
to purge the Prophet's kingdom.

from *EVERY WRONG DIRECTION*

D. M. Burt & Associates

In the middle of the road of life, I lost my way. Eight years I had laboured at law to marry a few years silence and slow time – three school, five practice – only to turn tail at the altar.

Liechtenstein was my last foreign trip for Touche Ross & Co. The second of my one-year contracts with them had ended early that summer of '75, and with it the obligation to develop the seedlings of an international tax department for their New York office. When I started for them, part time, two years earlier, the New York office had no international tax specialists; on my last day there it had five, and the practice was booming. In five years since leaving law school I'd saved enough to live comfortably for the next few years without earning; enough, I thought, to put tax regulations and Liechtenstein's virtual vaults behind and find out if I could write.

A six-string acoustic guitar leaned body down in a corner at Bass Rocks Lane, by a sliding glass door onto granite and sea. Morning coffee in hand, looking south-east over the chop to the horizon, I fancied myself picking it before a November fire, once I learned how. No law firm or corporate desk stood bare for me; my resumé lay in no hiring partner's briefcase; TR's last cheque had cleared, my taxes were paid, there was neither debt, wife, lover or child to mind. The $50,000 in my savings account would buy four scrimp-free years. Bridges burned, exits blocked, excuses exhausted, a pristine, portable, red Olivetti *Lettera* manual typewriter on my campaign desk, I had foreclosed all but writing.

Before I typed a word, two former clients called for advice, Denny Crispin, Boeing's tax director, and Marc Leduc, Northern Telecom's though both knew I'd been gone from TR for weeks. I figured they'd swallow no more than a few hours a month, pay me for my time what TR had charged them, and stretch savings but not filch writing hours. No non-compete barred me. *No brainer*, I thought, and shied at the first hedge. A few weeks later I fell at the second and did not try again for 30 years.

By the mid '70s the Gulf oil producers were issuing frequent international tenders for projects to modernise their countries, if not cultures. The second Saudi Five Year Economic Development Plan had teed-up the Kingdom to feverishly build roads, microwave towers, ports, schools, hospitals, housing, and office buildings to catapult its oases and mud-walled cities – Jeddah, Riyadh, Dharan – from 19th to 20th century in a half decade. Foreign contractors were to furnish the catapult.

TR clients began asking about Gulf business and tax laws, especially Arabia's, as the international tenders appeared. These queries often found their way to me, TR New York's international tax guru, and someone who at least could find Tehran and Riyadh on a globe. From pamphlets, articles, business guides, calls to TR affiliates in Arabia, Iran, the Emirates, Kuwait, and my four days in Tehran, I tried to answer them. The advice was often sketchy, *but in the kingdom of the blind, the one-eyed man is king.*

By fall 1975, America was nearly two years into a recession hallmarked by stagflation,[1] caused in large part by the Saudi jolt to oil prices. New England's contractors – road builders, construction companies – were especially hard hit; they slavered to win Saudi work. While I was still a consultant to TR, the New York office promised the Boston office that come fall I'd give a seminar for their clients on doing business in the Middle East. When the nights grew crisp, and though I'd left TR two months earlier, Boston asked me to honour that promise and I complied, thinking *Keep options open.*

The moon was yellow, and the leaves were falling,[2] and the conference room was packed. My 30-minute talk stretched to 90 as I took questions from some 50 contractors and exporters. Almost all were about Saudi Arabian agents, business laws, taxes, communications, visas, payment. Men, many with red necks and

---

1 Stagflation is when demand falls and prices rise steeply at the same time.
2 cf *Stagger Lee*, a black American folk song about gambling and murder. *The night was clear, and the moon was yellow/and the leaves came tumbling down.*

rough, browned fists of outdoor workers, rushed the dais when I finished, shoving business cards in my hand and asking for my phone number.

The surrounding crowd gave human form to the recession. This was not my first rodeo: one morning three years earlier, at San Francisco's St Francis Hotel, I'd spoken to near 1,500 financial executives, accountants and lawyers ravenous for details about DISC, Treasury's then new export subsidy. I promoted it to thousands more across America in the following months. Those exporters had been keen to hear me; the men encircling me this Boston autumn night almost in a swivet to hear what I had to say. These Yankee, Christian contractors, none of whom had worked outside their home state or region, were desperate enough for work to shoot crap in a desert peninsula more than three times the size of Texas, 6,500 miles and eight time zones away, that they knew nothing about; desperate enough to chance their companies in an Arabic speaking, nomadic Muslim monarchy with rudimentary communications and subject to Sharia law; desperate enough to rely for advice on a monoglot Jewish tax lawyer who'd made one four-day trip to Iran, and never been within 1,200 miles of Saudi Arabia. For some, it was build a Saudi road or school, or die.

At 8.30 a.m. next morning, Tuesday, at Bass Rocks Lane… *ring, ring, ring. Ring, ring…* at 6.50 p.m. that night. *Ring, ring, ring, ring…* through Friday afternoon. Some callers, when we spoke, complained the line was always busy. A week later New England companies hunting information on mid-East business rules still clogged my phone. As word spread of a Marblehead lawyer who knew about Levantine commercial and tax laws, calls came from further afield. My path diverged beside the sea.

I'd come to Marblehead to live a dream of the pen. All my short adult life, from first week at LaSalle College 15 years before, my heroes were writers, my hunger to join them. I believed writing one lyric poem that *pass[ed] into the memory of the race*[1] justifies a life, that making millions, billions, building commercial empires, ruling

---

1 My recollection is Yeats said this about his own poetry, but I've been unable to run the phrase down.

nations, doesn't; that one day with money and time enough I'd pursue this grail. So I'd told wives and lovers, so I'd told myself.

I'd rigged circumstances to force me to write. A winter rental on a spit of Massachusetts rock braving the North Atlantic might be a fine place to compose, *hunt and peck* good enough to draft a sonnet, but both useless for law practice. Bass Rocks had one phone line, no answering machine, no telex, no stationary, no secretary, and only me to research, draft documents, answer questions. Marblehead was a sailing town 17 miles north of Boston, not Wall Street. It lacked straw for the bricks of practice: pools of lawyers and legal secretaries from which to hire; case law reports, near-by law and commercial libraries. The internet for online research was a quarter century in the future.

The chalice shone before me. Ex- wives and lovers murmured *Do what you love.* Circumstances – youth, money, health – cleared the way. No one held a *Police Special*[1] to my temple and threatened *Keep practicing law or else.* But I'd already turned aside and taken the road more travelled. I told no caller *Sorry, I don't practice law anymore,* or *I'm on sabbatical.*

I covered every mirror I could in which I might see myself creeping down the road to practice. Rather than hunt for a secretary, I asked my part-time housekeeper, Bev Hower, if she could type. At her *Yes,* I hired her full time to answer the phone, type, and collect mail from my PO Box, as well as clean house. I installed no second phone line, no telex, hired no lawyer to help me, though already there was work for two. My mantra was *I'll handle this crush, pick up a quick few thousand, and in a few weeks reopen the Olivetti's case.* Deceit, all self-deceit.

Every practicing lawyer needs two things: stationary, for invoices if nothing else, and a system for recording billable time, the ineluctable hard evidence of private law practice. At my request Bev ordered both. The stationer asked what the letterhead should say, to prepare a proof. I scribbled *D. M. Burt & Associates* on a yellow pad, added the Bass Rocks' phone number and my PO Box, and handed it to Bev.

---

1   Colt Police Special – .38 calibre, six-round cylinder revolver. My Uncle Al carried a .38.

There were no *Associates*, the trade term for lawyers below partner level in a firm, there was no *D.M. Burt*. I never used my middle initial. The letterhead puffed a blastocyst practice, and its practitioner. My first thought in the morning, last at night remained *soon I'll pound that Olivetti*, but the mint letterheads and timesheets in my desk drawer gave that the lie. Within the month my dream lay buried at the back of a storage closet with the Olivetti and guitar.

On a Saturday morning a generation earlier, when I was 12 and a half years old and a butcher's apprentice at Pennsauken Meats, Marty Goldfield, my father's partner in the butcher shop, came into the back room where I was slicing boiled hams. He watched me whip slices from the stacker while the slicer ran, and platter them. After perhaps 30 seconds he said:

Danny, there's a nickel on the floor. I looked, saw nothing.
There, just in front of your shoe.
Marty, I can't see it.
Look, you're almost stepping on it.
Marty, there's no nickel.

He bent down and picked up a slice of ham from the sawdust covering the floor. *Danny, this is worth a nickel.* Shamed, face flushed, I stifled tears, washed the slice, added it to the platter and for the next 50 years picked up whatever fell but could still be sold.

The companies calling for advice were ham slices, money lying on the back-room floor. My father's tales of selling apples with his father on Depression-era street corners, of being beaten at 13 for buying a pair of new shoes with part of his first pay cheque; my nine years as a butcher boy at Pennsauken; tales of Jewish grief and hardship handed down from grandfather, to father, to me, were etched on my bones. My conditioned response was to let no ham slice lie.

If asked why I exploited the practice I'd stumbled on, rather than try to write as intended, I blamed childhood's indoctrinations. But the excuse was not the reason, just words to cover shame. Fear of being poor, the insecurity every post-Holocaust diaspora Jew feels, were not my dispositive terrors. Experience and history had scored me, sure, but in 1970s New England neither poverty nor pogrom was a real worry for a Cambridge educated, Yale trained, experienced lawyer with a modicum of capability and repute.

The bogeyman I fled lay ahead, not behind. He was the risk I would fail at the only thing I loved; he was the fear of defeat on my only field of dreams. I'd *chickened out*, knew it, and was mortified. From the day Bev ordered *D. M. Burt & Associates* letterhead until I gave law up three decades later, if a stranger asked *What do you do?* I'd hesitate, mumble *A bit of business,* and change the subject.

The Cessna 340 rolled to a stop a football pitch away from Logan's private air terminal. Two men deplaned almost before the chocks were set and walked towards the terminal: one, fair-skinned, heavyset, six foot plus, with thin, stringy hair and the dry, red-scabbed skin of an eczemic, the other swarthy, chunky, with thick, curly hair and a head shorter, both mid-50s. It was late morning, last Sunday in November 1975, as I waited for them inside the terminal's tarmac door.

The big WASP was Tom Dunbar, CEO of R.P. DeSantis, Inc., a New York road builder; the short Italian Tony Salvei, CFO. In the '50s DeSantis had paved a fair portion of the roads and airport runways in eastern New York state and southern Connecticut, but fell on hard times. Tom and Tony were running the company when the founder died in the mid '60s, and bought it cheap from his heirs. Tony had called Bass Rocks Lane 24 hours earlier to introduce himself and ask to meet next day.

DeSantis was paving little in New England as we shook hands. In one of the terminal's private meeting rooms Tom said they'd been to Saudi Arabia a few months earlier, appointed a Saudi agent, al-Mohsin Establishment, tendered on a Saudi Ministry of Transport road contract, and a few days ago received a telex saying they'd won. They were returning to Jeddah three days after New Year to sign it and mobilise for construction, and asked me to go with them to deal with problems they were having with their Saudi agent, as well as create a legal framework to avoid US taxes on their hoped-for Saudi profits.

You needed a visa to visit Saudi, and the application required two things I hadn't, a Saudi sponsor and a religion. Al-Mohsin supplied the first, the second was my problem. My grandfather and father were atheists, though strong ethnic Jews, as was I. If called yid, kike or sheeny I'd fight, but did not observe Jewish holidays, eschew gentile lovers and wives, or know a rabbi who would supply a good standing certificate. I also doubted the Saudi embassy would look kindly on an application with *Jewish* in its *Religion* space. After a brief call with Tony's visa expediter, and a $100 donation, I became a Unitarian, whatever that was, shielded by my atheism from apostasy and tribal guilt.

Arrivals Hall, Jeddah, 3 January 1976. It had been scarf and gloves weather – 0°C, de minimis humidity – 20 hours and 6,000 miles ago at Boston's Logan. It was T-shirt and shorts weather – 20°C, 50 percent humidity – and nearly midnight, as men in expensive business suits, or spotless white thobes, swinging Connolly leather briefcases emerged from the forward door of our L-1011 from London. From the rear doors poured stained, coarse thobes and burqas, many lugging plunder from London shopping sprees in large cloth sacks or cardboard boxes. The sticky tarmac between plane and terminal was dark; passengers left the pool of harsh halogen light from construction lamps at the base of the stairs, and shuffled cautiously, single file, toward what looked like a warehouse. I peeled off my sweater as my feet hit the ground and straggled with them, jet-lagged, into the Arrivals Hall.

Between Arrivals Hall doors and Passport Control was, nothing – no baggage carousels, no signs identifying areas for luggage from arriving flights, no baggage trolleys, no uniformed porters, only grey, stained cement floor and foot wide steel columns supporting the roof. Fluorescent ceiling lights spread a green, ghastly glow over dyspeptic knots of the deplaned. The thobes and burqas waited fatalistically for luggage to appear, some of the men telling prayer beads. The suits sweated, paced, peered into the black on the tarmac.

From time to time scrawny fellahin in dingy thobes and sandals dragged baggage carts into the hall, piled with luggage high as they could throw a bag. They picked an empty spot on the terminal's floor, dumped the luggage so it formed a small hill, and straggled back to open cargo holds for more.

The passengers gathered round the baggage handlers like maggots on road kill and peered at the luggage hills as they rose, looking for a familiar strap, tag, or material. If you spotted your bag you shoved through the milling crowd to rip it free; if you didn't, you clambered up the hill in search of it.

We reached our hotel at 1 a.m. It was the height of the Saudi building boom, a gold rush for recycling petrodollars, Jeddah what San Francisco had been in 1849.[1] Our packed plane was one of four crammed international flights landed there that night. The hotel, the best in town, was the equal of a Times Square whore-hostel renting rooms by the hour. Several western businessmen were asleep on couches in the moss green tiled reception area. There was no bell-hop. Our reservations were lost until Tom helped the night clerk search the reservations ledger for them, using a $100 bill as a pointer. My clients went to their rooms to sleep; I to mine to work.

Earlier that day, after lunch on our flight from London, Tony had handed me a copy of DeSantis' agency agreement with al-Mohsin. Twenty minutes later I kneel beside his seat and tell him the agreement has three clauses that put deSantis at al-Mohsin's mercy. First, al-Mohsin has the right to receive road building payments due deSantis from the Transport Ministry, deduct its commission then pass on the balance to deSantis. If deSantis and al-Mohsin disagree on something, al-Mohsin can withhold the balance from deSantis. Second, Sharia law applied by a Saudi court governs the contract, rather than ICC arbitration.[2] Third, al-Mohsin will hold the passports of deSantis' in-country employees. Saudi agents had used foreign employees as bargaining chips in disputes with their employers by preventing them from leaving the Kingdom. *Tony, this contract's commercial suicide. You've got to renegotiate it.*

That's your job, Dan.

Across the table will be Raymond Nakachian, aka Raymond Nash, al-Mohsin general manager; 43 years old, Lebanese, polyglot (Arabic, English, French, German, Russian) charismatic, and notorious. It was customary for non-Saudis – Lebanese, Syrians,

---

1 James Marshall discovered gold at Sutter's Mill in 1848, The California gold rush followed as the news slowly spread, and by 1849 San Francisco was morphing from a sleepy pacific coastal village to a city.

2 Substantial international contracts customarily provide that disputes shall be resolved in a neutral country under the Rules of the International Chamber of Commerce.

most often Palestinians – to manage international and daily admin of a Saudi agency's business. These managers spoke English as well as Arabic, often French and German, were cosmopolitan, experienced international businessmen, and loyal only to money.

Their employers, the agency owners, often spoke only Arabic, had little if any education, were un-travelled, and, in at least one case was illiterate. They managed the Saudi side of things – securing contracts, permits, visas, and assuring government agencies paid on time. Saudi law required every foreign company working in the Kingdom to hire one.

The local agent ostensibly guided foreign principals in local ways, supplied admin and logistical help, and kept them in line in-country. But Saudi agents had neither staff nor expertise to help foreign contractors execute contracts. Builders supplied their own expertise, equipment, and personnel. King Fahd's government didn't need the agents to control foreign contractors. Ministry contracts gave the government ample rights and power, and once a contractor's personnel and equipment were in the Kingdom the government had all the leverage it needed. So, what did agents do for their commissions?

They arranged and paid the bribes necessary to procure contracts. A standard Saudi agent's commission was five percent of contract value, e.g. $2.5m on a $50m contract. There was no maximum; commissions were often 10 percent or higher, depending on contract size; I've seen them breast 25 percent. The worldwide rule of thumb for the percentage of a contract an in-country representative agent is due, is the higher a contract's value the lower the agent's percentage, since the agent does roughly the same amount of work for a $50m as for a $500m contract. The reverse was true in Saudi; the higher the contract's value, the larger the agent's percentage. This anomaly spotlit the agent's true role; commissions in Saudi and other Near Eastern countries were higher the greater the contract value because the more a contract was worth, the more senior the Ministry employees, and more of them, who had to be paid off.

Agents implied, sometimes bragged, that much of their commission went for bribes. Foreign principals rarely witnessed a bribe being paid, but circumstantial evidence argued they were. Agents supplied no admin services, office space, housing, or employees to contractors to justify their commissions. Gulf country government employees and kin stayed at Paris' Ritz and London's Dorchester hotels, shopped at Chanel and Versace, Givenchy and Hermes, Graff and Boodles, Huntsman and Tommy Nutter, whose suites, scents, silks, sparklers and suits no government employee's salary in the world could have paid for. Experience, logic, local lore and Levantine commercial culture testified the agent's function was to bribe.

Dawn broke as I added the last words to a revised agency agreement for deSantis. A chant floated across the rooftops of the two- and three-storey buildings below and through my open window. I couldn't make out the words, or for a few seconds guess what it was. Then the sound raised an echo from boyhood of synagogue chazans leading diaspora faithful in high holiday prayers, and I realised it was a muezzin calling flock of another faith to sunrise hosannas. Ever after Jeddah felt less foreign than the clay tennis courts and parquet dance floors of New England's WASP yacht clubs.

I went for a run through ancient Jeddah's shattered streets to clear my head. Within a few strides I was weaving through hordes of honking, careening, white Toyota flatbed pick-ups, like a striker through defenders; 40 years later television viewers around the world became familiar from ISIS videos with these same middle-eastern workhorses, 50 calibres rather than rebars behind their cabs. Wooden framing planks, cement sacks, steel cabling, gas cylinders for welding torches, chains, compressors, jackhammers, Yemeni, Somali and Pakistani labourers in kaffiyehs, bounced on their heaving cargo beds. Piles of concrete, steel, and plastic pipes were heaped on every street. Yellow Komatsu and Caterpillar back-hoes, mobile cranes, and tractors jostled for space in a competition it looked like Komatsu was winning. Rolls of steel cable, plastic water and waste piping, electrical conduit cable were strewn amongst portable generators, lumber piles and concrete mixers.

Passing heavy equipment had un-cobbled streets, where they hadn't been excavated to lay pipe, pour foundations, or replace open sewers with buried conduits. Craters gaped where once houses stood, flanked by half demolished mud walls. Newsreel footage of London's East End during the Blitz spooled through my mind. The stuttering *pow! pow! pow!* of jackhammers followed by the *whoosh! whoosh! whoosh!* of exhaling compressors driving them, soprano screams of power saws and drills, grunt of tractor diesels, crash of falling walls, builders' shouts and curses combined in a cacophony that forced would-be speakers to shout. Diesel fumes mingling with dust from demolished buildings and excavations, and stink from open sewers fouled the air. It was 7 a.m., work in full swing.

Jeddah's harbour was clogged with ships waiting to offload heavy equipment and building supplies, the wharves piled to impassibility with freight waiting to be cleared. The demand from foreign contractors for *ro-ros,* roll on-roll off ships which could land cargo on the beaches of Obhur Creek, twenty-two miles north of the city beyond the choked harbour, propelled international *ro-ro* charter prices stratospheric.

Jeddah was not unique; construction convulsed all Arabia. The Saudi masses looked on silently as foreign contractors demolished and rebuilt their cities, flouted their customs, ridiculed and disdained them. Four years later, in November 1979, those silent witnesses applauded Wahabi fundamentalists who seized the *Masjid al-Haram,* the Grand Mosque in Mecca, the Muslim world's holiest site, and lit the blue paper for the Muslim fundamentalist explosion whose shock-waves daily rattle the world.

Tom, Tony and I arrive at 9 a.m., on schedule, at al-Mohsin Establishment to meet Raymond. He arrives at 11, then keeps us waiting another half hour. When I complain, Tony tells me Saudi businessmen turning up hours late for meetings, always unapologetic, is usual in Kingdom. Business in Kingdom, he explains, is done the IBM way: *Inshallah* (God willing), *Bokra* (tomorrow), *Malesh* (no problem). One of these three words was the invariable, interchangeable reply to questions such as when a meeting would begin, a payment made, a shipment cleared. *When will Raymond get here? An hour, Inshallah. When will the ministry pay our last invoice? Bokra. Can you clear our bulldozer through customs today? Malesh.* But God was often unwilling, tomorrow never came, and every clearance proved a problem.

Raymond was medium height, with a refrigerator's build, shaved head, snarling voice, penchant for bragging about his karate black belt; he swaggered, was abrupt and given to shouting at and cursing subordinates. Calumny became him. He's railing about *that sand-nigger*, his dark-skinned boss and al-Mohsin's owner, Sheik Mohammad, when we enter his office near noon. It was the first time I'd heard the slur, ironic as Raymond was dun-olive coloured himself; dark skin apparently is an affliction even in a khaki-hued land. Twelve years earlier in London, as Raymond Nash, he owned El Condor Club with Peter Rachman, the eponymous slumlord.[1] There royals, toffs, and politicians mingled with showgirls and models like Christine Keeler[2] and Mandy Rice Davies, criminals like the Kray brothers, and Russian spies in the stew that became the Profumo scandal[3]; Raymond was reputed a money and gambling man, something of a heavy, in the mix.

Tom introduces me as deSantis' lawyer, says I have concerns about the agency agreement, and resiles. I begin *There are problems with the agreement…* Raymond cuts me off. *Come back tonight*, he barks, then hollers for someone to show us out.

Most serious business with agents in Arabia is done after dinner, between 10 p.m. and 1 a.m. Their offices are too chaotic, interruptions too constant for serious negotiation during office hours. An hour before midnight Tom and Tony sit either corner of a large, deep, knackered sofa in Raymond's office, me between them. Raymond presides from a leather chair opposite. A coffee table almost as long as our sofa, heaped with papers, separates the parties.

There are no pleasantries. I tell Raymond the agreement has three unacceptable terms: al-Mohsin's right to receive deSantis' payments from the Ministry; retention of deSantis' staff's passports; governing Saudi law, as well as a number of minor faults. I reach into

---

1 Peter Rachman, a Holocaust survivor and resistance fighter, came to the UK from Poland in 1948. Infamous for renting slum flats at outrageous rents, his surname became an English noun for heartless slumlord. Both Christine Keeler and Mandy Rice-Davies were at one time or another his mistress.

2 See Christine Keeler's memoir, *Secrets and Lies*, ch. 5, and the Profumo scandal.

3 In 1963 UK Tory and Secretary of State for War, John Profumo, admitted to sharing the favours of Christine Keeler with a Russian spy. Profumo resigned, and the Tories lost the general election a year later.

my briefcase for the revised contract to hand to Raymond when he shouts

No! You signed it; the deal's done. Who the fuck do you think you are? This meeting's over!

Tom and Tony blanch, press their spines and sides against their respective sofa corners as if to pass through them to anywhere else, say nothing.

Raymond, I've told my clients they can't work under this contract; they'll leave Saudi first.

He sits wordlessly for perhaps thirty seconds, leans slightly towards me, says softly *You know, Saudi's a dangerous place. Something might happen to you, maybe walking back to your hotel tonight…* As he speaks he pushes some of the papers off the coffee table to expose what might be a Beretta.

C'mon Raymond. If I go missing, you'll be the first person questioned. I'm an American, and the Saudis will care a hell of a lot more about what happens to me than they will about you. Here's the revised contract. We can discuss it tomorrow.

We rise, leave; Tom and Tony are silent on the short walk to our hotel. I'd seen killers since I could recognise faces; my uncle Al was one, a hitman. A .38 hung by its trigger guard on a nail below the till at my father's 4th street butcher shop; a .22 lay in the top drawer of his bedroom dresser. I played with the .22 when no one was home. Raymond is no killer, at least not in Saudi Arabia. He signs the contract, unchanged, the next day.

CONTRASTS

Matinée

But Paradise is locked and bolted,
and the cherubim stands behind us.
                On the Marionette Theatre,
                Heinrich von Kleist (translated by Idris Parry)

Crouched in a punt prow closing
on a limestone landing, by lawns
ancient in Wordsworth's time, the don's
daughter in jeans tenses to spring.
Thud, scramble up the bank, unlatch
an iron wicket, and she's loose,
an ingénue flustering goose
and grebe on gravel, grass, mud patch,
the groundlings at her prepubescent
play. We dog her, clap, warn, wave,
meander under architrave
and round the Backs, two senescent
men at dusk punting in Eden.

Martha, Mary and Magdalene Retouched

For Paula Rego

In the left panel, Martha sits,
thighs akimbo on a tall stool,
pastels open by bare right foot,
eyes raised, brush poised to put
on canvas cruelty, fear, rape;
not Rossetti's ethereal amateur,
but novice worthy of the ur-sister
who told off Christ, and maybe,
set him to washing-up after tea.

A woman cradles a man
in the centre painting, a Pieta
unlike Michelangelo's five centuries ago
in cream Carrara; no Mary bowed,
bearing her son on Golgotha
but frowning, ramrod, tempered lady,
on her knees a tall, thin, pasty body
in boxer shorts, a male too old
to be her child, her look too cold
to be a mother's, more like the stare
of the jilted lover
watching Aeneas bear away into the north.

The story ends with image pulled
from cinquecento Dutch devotional,
The Magdalen Reading:
lime robe neck to toes,
white head scarf, bible,
cabinet against her back,
changed to pleated, knee-length skirt,
unzipped Barbour, plum beret,
battered, ransacked, Churchill case
bracing the reader's carapace,
thick-soled, black calf-length boots;
a seated gypsy in a *conte moral* –
life shrunk to clothes on your back,
a bare room, a paperback.

Three modern saints
for an atheist's wall,
pastels on paper on aluminium,
unsex the Gospels
with the painter's autobiography.

London Contemporary

He shows up half drunk, and half hour late,
picks his teeth through every course,
downs a *Negroni*, two chardonnays,
five cabernets, two ports;
by his plate places a phone
the way hit men lay a gun
by their thigh when they drive alone,
and fields four calls before we're done;
mentions his stable's stars –
Lucian, Gerhardt, Bridget, Cy –
not what makes them what they are,
but who's fetched what and why;
and last, turns to collectors bagged
at fairs and galas on six continents:
She's what she has, he quips,
and *They're both tasteless pricks.*

Once he was courtly, when Persephone's
gnawed pomegranate, Ophelia's splayed
hair, Cupid candle-lit by Psyche
were his vespers and dealing not his trade.

Bukhara

Backlit by the sun
on a boulevard in Teheran,
a tribesman tottered towards us,
rolled rug over his shoulder.

Three years his daughters
wove, knotted and cut the threads
he lugged from Turkmenistan
to raise money for the Hajj.

Spread at our feet, five wool rows
of octagons, flecked with terracotta
berry-dyed a molten lava,
fixed the eye within the selvage.

I bought it for those colours;
witless, laid them in a skylight parlour,
where sunshine bled to beige
the palette that entranced me.

Only a thin black band stood fast
around each pale polygon
marching in field and borders
like pilgrims circling the Ka'aba.

In that swarm I glimpsed the faith
that propelled the weavers' fingers,
sallow flags in a faded token
praising a power beyond my ken.

The Greatest Generation

for Sam Hynes

He walks like a lamplighter through my mind,
in the brown bomber jacket he wore
over whites and to class in the fall,
Marine Corps issue from late '44,
when he flew Hellcats at Mindinao.

A line that day, *Her beauty, like a bent
bow*, loosed him on misremembering,
how it scrapes and daubs at memories
and paints a past we wish had been,
how when he was a teen
he recalled a lament for Carnival,
So we'll go no more a roving
as *rowing*, and took it to heart as pastoral:
eight sweatered Ivy League athletes
at dusk, oars upright,
shouldering their shell to its rack for the night.

A shot cut short his reverie.
Two flights down in the parking lot
we gather, hear... *Dallas... lie in state...*
on his car's radio, news from the spot,
go back, pack papers, silently separate.

We watched the slow march of caisson, coffin,
captain-less horse, black-veiled woman,
then went on as before,
though he mothballed the jacket won in the war.

November 9, 2016

Caliban clove the fetters
that hobbled the people of hate,
sprung Stars & Bars, and howls
of *White Power! Immigrants Out!*
brayed *Lock her up!* through the agora,
and dismembered the moral order.

The sun did not explode,
wind groomed the trees
and buried gutters under leaves,
lobsters scrabbled from littorals
to deeper, warmer offshore seas,
no instrument distinguished the day
sixty-three million Americans
blew illusions about them away.

In the gathering shadows
the outer dark takes stock
of tribal loathing, tribal fear
that gnaw heartland and its Kaiser,
cockroaches in the gene,
primeval, ugly, adamantine
that spy an enemy in every stranger,
twin vandals, that for a lark torch a hijab
while its wearer hails a Yellow cab.
And in sum, we are afraid.

SALVAGES

Who He Was

i.m. Joe Burt 1915–1995

The skeleton in a wheelchair props rented
tackle on the rail, stares down twenty feet
from a pier through salt subtropical air
at shoal water wavelets for blue slashes
flashing toward the bait below his float,
and misses one hit, two, a third, an inept
young butcher far from inner city streets
recovering from surgery, too proud
to bask with codgers, too weak to walk or swim,
a sutured rag-doll whose one permitted
sport is dangling blood worms from a pole.

His father's plumb and adze, mother's thread and pins,
tradesmen, carters, peddlers, kaftaned bearded
kin, village landsmen from Ukraine, friends, nothing
in his life smelled of ocean; but cleaver
held again, he kept on fishing. Once a week
he drove eighty miles east to prowl the sea
with charter-men, ever farther from the coast
till, white coat and meat hook junked, he trolled
ballyhoo for marlin eight hours run offshore.

Two score years and four skiffs on, by his command
we laid him down in fishing clothes, khaki
trousers, khaki shirt, *Dan-Rick* on the right
breast pocket, on the left *Capt. J. Burt.*

For John Crook

i.m. 1921–2007

Punts gone from the Backs,
courts cleared by Christmas, only swans
and caped choirboys leave tracks
where the winter of his words immures a don
indifferent to honours,
but not his College, or its scholars.

We he fostered would physic
what departs, but discover
we're still charges. Shamed by catheter
from gut to turn-up draining waste,
by wheelchair at his staircase door
for hauls beyond the gates,
he croaks *No! I am decaying.,*
down the phone
to shoo comforters away,
a classicist dying alone
behind a sported oak,
slumped by a gas fire in an armchair,
skin sloughed from mandible and thighs,
reading Georgian poetry to bear
decay's degenerate surprise.

We must prepare, nearing his set,
for clarinet stilled, twinkle fled;
prepare, should he permit a visit,
and feign not to notice what's unsaid.

Speechless

He was selling seconds
to sweatshop tailors
when they drafted him to war;
bolts of Bradford worsteds,
Newberry long fibre cottons,
Levi denims, Dupont rayons,
peddled on both shoulders
down Yiddish speaking alleys,
and cobbled eighteenth century streets.

A faded de-mob photo
shows him home a hero –
laughing wife and her best friend
nestled in either arm
below his emoji smile,
pairs of one-inch silver bars
pinned where his inventory sat –
weeks before he learned
his only child
was deaf and dumb.

He lived life in retreat after that,
in his warehouse behind eight-foot high
mill-end stacks, can't-see
to can't-see six days a week;
sign language beyond his ken;
wife never pregnant again;
and no talk of his silent daughter
while we chummed stripers
on Barnegat Bay,
as if, like soiling yourself,
she was something shameful to say.

Manicure

i.m. R.M.P. (1938–2015)

They stitched him into all they did,
gatherings, holidays, vacation trips,
and went weekly to the care-home
where he'd been sent to live,
grown too big for a parent to lift:
Let me see your nails, dear;
Show us your talons, son;
clippings plink in a bowl, and after,
perhaps, a push about the grounds.
But they were unsure
with him slumped in his wheelchair,
speech gnarled, neurons
tangled more each year,
what from week to week he recalled of them,
or when they came no more, would comprehend.

The widow rolls him to the corpse,
touches his finger to its lips,
then helps him lay a lily
on the rib cage boxed in rush,
that cold skin may help him understand
why now only one will visit him.

Two sit in his room, where three had been:
Let me see your nails, dear, she begins.
No, her child says, *show talons*.

Homage for a Waterman

i.m. Holmes Russell

He jams clam tongs down three feet
and fetches bottom, pulls them so wide
he's spread-eagled over the bay,
scissors back, heaves till knuckles meet,
and hoists the bales over the side,
squinting for little necks or oysters,
a black stick figure in oil-skins
pile driving in November sleet.

Townies charter him to cast the bars
with bucktail lures, or eels, a year's
bookings complete before the season starts,
and find him on the dock at dawn
in white sweat shirt, khakis, red
and black plaid lumber jacket,
a Triton skippers heed
on where to run, what baits to work.

Thirty years ago time took his boat,
in due course him, and his parties.
Where he rests, under stone, urn,
I never learned.
The ten-year-old who begged to help
his hero lift the hook
wears titanium knees for bone.
But when winds sough, and seagulls toy
with thermals off my hollowed cliff,
Holmes leathered face looms into sight
through boom and spray, helm held tight,
bow-on to breakers in the bight.

Lament for Grace

i.m. Frederic Close Towers (1934–2016)

A shuttered Down East cottage,
beached float, on the sea-wall
four white Adirondacks, toll for the season,
and octogenarian who summered here.
Today, locals cellar the chairs
and stow him beside the weathered graves
of his first love Kay, and their only child.

He was a lodestone for neighbours,
friends, family at the violet hour;
they gathered on this harbour porch
to sit, sip and rehearse distractions –
highballs, gossip, high-tech
gadgets he was first to test,
shared right-wing shibboleths.

Bored by tech-toys, chatter and gin,
I came for the heart of him, like a beast
to a salt lick; for his open-armed shout
Why, hello there, Brother Dan!
when I walked in,
as if my hand clutched a princely gift,
or cure for his cancer-ridden wife.

No common caste or custom drew us close,
our politics and faiths stood toe to toe,
yet like the rest I could not choose but go
and bide by one of nature's innocents,
watch chutes strain homeward up Soames Sound,
and salvage, for a twilight, the hope I had
as a boy off-shore mating for Dad.

Deposition

i. *Tumour*

Surgeons probed the ruin
that six weeks ago was a woman
for the source of her Nile of pain:
razed ovaries through a keyhole –
they proved benign;
twice hoovered her guts
through a nasogastric hose –
but still they fouled;
slit the abdomen at last
and from her colon cut
the egg-sized ruby mass
that damned her bowels.

ii. *Post-Op*

In the room scrubs come and go,
check vital signs, the glucose drip,
bring clear liquids for her to sip,
but tell us nothing we want to know.

Either side of the bed we stand,
spin bad news into bland,
walk off at times to hide
trembling lip, dampening eye,
and dread the 'path' report
will ferry hope to Hell.

Mid-morning, mid-afternoon,
the scarecrow hanging on my arm
shuffles speechless round the ward
while I hum *Va pensiero* under my breath,
conjure the orchestra, hear
Nabucco's Hebrew slaves implore
a God I'm certain is not there,
for strength to endure.

iii. *Delphi*

Nine storeys up the January sun
fills the oncology waiting rooms,
lights pear wood chairs,
beige carpets, off-white walls,
and pencil-thin, pale alopetes,
whose cadaverous flesh
mocks the studied calmness.
Patient, daughter, and I sit,
fidget, prattle, go for a pee,
and feign no fear
the news will be
not what we want to hear.

The haruspex enters quietly,
half-tied surgical gown askew,
scuffed, brown wing-tipped shoes,
a shambling, portly, distant man
whose blank face, guarded gaze,
say he's acted the raven in too many plays:

You have Stage IV colon cancer. We couldn't find the source.
The surgeon who removed the blockage thinks he got it all,
but can't be sure.
When you recover a little more, we'll do an endoscopy,
and PET scan; but I doubt they'll change our view. Chemotherapy's
standard for what you have,
a six-months course, if you can stand it.
Then we review.

What will the chemo do?

Give you a year, maybe two…

Her late-life only child turns aside to sob;
I flinch, though the verdict's no surprise;
and my wasted, high school heart-throb,
poleaxed, mute, empty eyed,
decouples from us and, like a stranger,
boards her little black train.

iv. *Totentanz*

Death settles on the exam table
as the oncologist bids good-day,
flutters anthracite feathers,
eyes us, then with a nod
swings his new partner away.

Wrapped in his grim wingspan
gyring down the shadow path,
she pries at the talons
that clamp her fast,
with chemicals, diet, all she can muster
to loosen them for a measure,
though nothing can ever dissever
this pair from their round together.

I am a wallflower at the dance
watching a lady slowly die,
and as sigh treads on sigh
replay a sixty-year-old teen romance.

v. *Coda*

She paused, looking at him for a moment with a smile.
'My name? I am Mademoiselle Yvonne de Galais...'
> *Then she was gone.*
> > *Le Grand Meaulnes*, Alain Fournier

We trudged under the lash of measurement,
each pulse a question,
Will the next scan be clear?
pursued by odds we'd too soon hear
Your cancer is past treatment.

Against that hour I sifted memory
for the clarity a tango with extinction brings:
not the last ten winter years
when we grew close,
chance-met again after half a century,
but three months as your subject
while you slummed it,
a pubescent uptown rose
dallying with a bit of rough.

I refined myself
after that brief encounter,
quarried Wordsworth, Eliot, Lowell, Yeats,
cast your deities as mine,
pictured us kneeling at their shrine,
but the conjunctive moment past
worshipped alone.

I'll sing no sad songs for you,
my dearest, now you are dead,
instead for *kaddish* will surrender
the rage loving you engendered
and the still-born dreams that drove me
lee-rail buried down the years.

Jill Rubinson
i.m. 17.08.1943 – 30.07.2018

Notes

Every Wrong Direction – The second part of the prose memoir, excerpts from which have appeared in *PN Review*.

'Thief' – *chains* was short for *chain stores*, the local supermarkets owned or franchised by the national food retailers. Every chain store had a butcher shop in it, which because of the chains' greater buying power often could buy meat cheaper than could small independent stores like my father's, and sell it cheaper as well.
Schvitz (Yiddish for *to sweat*) was the slang name for the Camac Baths, a Russian bath house in centre city which Philadelphia's Jewish workers and tradesmen like my father frequented at the end of their work week to steam and knead the fatigue from their bones.

'Impostor Syndrome' – Institute is the Institute for Advanced Study in Princeton, New Jersey.

'Familiars' – Freeport-McMoran, a sulphur miner founded in Freeport, Texas in 1912, now the world's largest mining and mineral producer, was headquartered in New Orleans, Louisiana in 1971. Senator Russell B. Long, senior senator from Louisiana, was Chairman of the Senate Finance Committee, the Senate committee responsible for income taxes, at the time the events in 'Familiars' occurred.

'Prospecting' – In October 1973 Saudi Arabia and the other members of the OPEC-embargoed oil sales to countries supporting Israel in the Yom Kippur war. The resulting *oil shock* quadrupled oil prices from $3 to $6 in 12 months.

'Departure' – On 29 November 1979, Saudi fundamentalists seized the *Masjid al-Haram*, called the Grand Mosque, in Mecca and called for the overthrow of the House of Saud. After the Saudi government regained control of the mosque King Khalid implemented much stricter enforcement of Sharia, or Muslim religious law, and fundamentalist power in the Kingdom waxed.

'Singing School' – A *rock* is trader slang for a million of any currency. *Acronyms* refers to trader terms for financial items, e.g. *bps* for basis points, *CDO* for collateralised debt obligation, *BOSS* for bond and option sales strategy.

'Heeps' – Uriah Heep, a sycophantic, ambitious, avaricious, loathsome clerk in Dickens' *David Copperfield.*

'Martha, Mary and Mary Magdalene, Retouched' – Anthony Rudolph commissioned and printed this ekphrastic poem along with other commissioned works as an eightieth birthday tribute for Paula Rego.

'Lament for Grace' – A *chute* is sailor's slang for a spinnaker, the large, traditionally bulbous, light sail used when sailing downwind.